ZINY'S DRIVING SCHOOL

BY

LYNN HEFELE

ILLUSTRATED

BY

FRANK SCICCHITANO

Ziny's Driving School

All rights reserved. No part of this publication may be used or reproduced in any manner whatsoever without written permission.

Manufactured in the United States of America

For information, please contact:

LEPE, Inc.

3 Griggs Drive

Greenlawn, NY 11740

www.LEPEinc.com

631-626-9190

ISBN-13: 978-0615-51107-8

LCCN: 2011913904

Illustrator contact information:

Frank Scicchitano

www.tanoart.com

Author contact information:

Lynn Hefele

lynn.hefele@gmail.com

Copyright ©2010, 2014

Dedication and Acknowledgements

To My Husband Steve…Love You!

I want to thank the Huntington School District for their support of my vision to develop Literature Enhanced Physical Education. I especially want to express my appreciation to Joe Giani, Margaret Evers, and Georgia McCarthy for encouraging me to follow my passion.

I would like to express my sincerest appreciation to Frank Scicchitano for creating Ziny and all her pals. As an artist, his professionalism, creativity, and commitment to artistic excellence is unsurpassed.

Thanks to Stephen Coulon, Professor of Physical Education, Springfield College and Mara Manson, Associate Professor of Physical Education, Adelphi University, for critiquing the lessons created for Ziny's adventure, as well as, Carol Deren and Shasank Munim for helping to edit and typeset the manuscript.

Special thanks go to the children of Jefferson Primary and Karen Fischer for bringing Ziny to life in the gymnasium. Their imagination and enthusiasm transformed the story into a delightful and meaningful educational experience.

Finally, to my husband Steve, and my boys Harrison and TJ, I would like to express my heartfelt appreciation for your continued support of this ongoing project. I could not do it without you.

Ziny had been waiting for this day her whole life! It was the first day of driving school.

It seemed as though she would never reach 9 years old and grow to the 52 inches that was required for flying.

Then almost overnight, she grew a whopping 13 inches with just 2 days before her 9th birthday. Today was going to be great!

Ziny put on her brand new driving helmet and her fuzzy new mittens and headed off to flying school with her dad.

Most of her friends were there with their spaceships. Some of them had been flying for almost a year but some were beginners just like her.

She wouldn't get her permanent flying license until she turned ten and completed a safe flying course. Some of her friends were eleven and still had not passed the test!

Ziny's dad left her at the gate and she joined the other students waiting for the instructor. She stood with her friend Zander marveling over all the beautiful Quasars in the parking lot.

There were many sizes and shapes to choose from as well as ones that were meant for speed or distance. Ziny picked out a pink Quasar with purple bumpers and a silver jet engine.

Ziny would get a droid as an instructor. No living creature was allowed in a spaceship with a new driver. Her droid's name was Teacha. She was made of polished silver chrome and had a shiny dome with pink trim. Ziny thought she went nicely with the colors of her new Quasar.

Teacha's job was to make sure Ziny understood all of the safety rules. Accidents almost never happened but on those occasions when there was a crash, the driver would have to turn in their Quasar for repairs. That meant your lesson was over for the day.

Ziny and Teacha found their Quasar and got inside buckling up their seat belts. Teacha explained that safe flying meant always keeping your self-space.

She told Ziny to pretend there was a big bubble around her and to keep everything far enough away so that it wouldn't pop.

Next, they checked the mirrors and landing gear, and started up the engine. Boing, boing, went the ship bouncing up and down moving forward slowly. "Check your turbines, Ziny, you are in jumping gear," said Teacha.

Ziny shifted into 1st gear and her ship slowly moved forward. The speed limit on the intercity spaceway was 25 miles per hour (mph).

This speed was used for beginners and crowded spaces. Ziny quickly mastered 1st gear with Teacha giving out the commands: left, right, high, low, and zigzag.

Ziny thought driving was simple but suddenly everything went black! Ziny was frightened. "Stay calm and spin the wheel," said Teacha in a calm voice. "You slipped into a black hole. Spinning out of it is simple and fun." Ziny slowly turned the wheel and began twirling back to the surface. "Nicely done!" said Teacha. "Now let's try that jumping gear you were in earlier."

"Jumping gear is particularly good for the meteor zone and the Space Zoo," advised Teacha. Ziny switched into jumping gear just as she came to an "Alien Crossing" sign.

Groups of Martians were walking their dogs and Ziny practiced hopping, jumping, and leaping over them. Boing, boing, boing went her turbines. What great fun!

"Shift into 2nd gear," said Teacha. Ziny moved the stick into 2nd gear and began cruising at 50 mph. Fifty miles per hour was used for neighborhoods with fewer spaceships on the airways.

Teacha taught her how to swerve and change levels while always looking out for other ships. She taught her the gallop and the slide which she used for squeezing into small spaces and passing slow moving space trucks.

"Now into 3rd gear," commanded Teacha. Third gear made Ziny nervous. Seventy-five mph was scary!

They would have to get on the interspace highway to go this fast. Sometimes people were reckless at this speed because they forgot that they could only go one way.

"It is important to keep a safe distance from other ships and follow the directions at all times because accidents at this speed could get someone hurt," said Teacha.

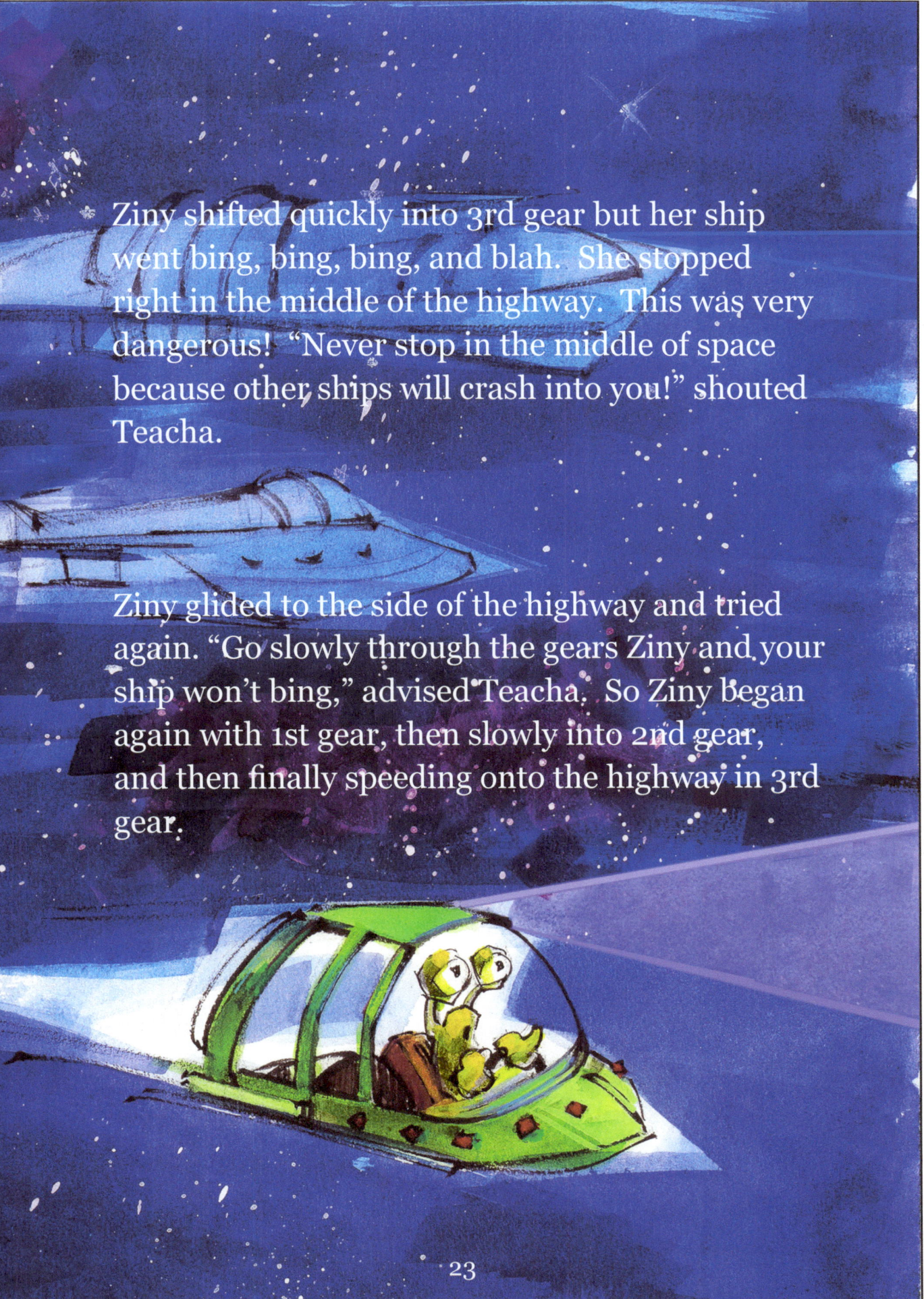

Ziny shifted quickly into 3rd gear but her ship went bing, bing, bing, and blah. She stopped right in the middle of the highway. This was very dangerous! "Never stop in the middle of space because other ships will crash into you!" shouted Teacha.

Ziny glided to the side of the highway and tried again. "Go slowly through the gears Ziny and your ship won't bing," advised Teacha. So Ziny began again with 1st gear, then slowly into 2nd gear, and then finally speeding onto the highway in 3rd gear.

"Ziny, it's time to end our lesson for today," said Teacha. "But we haven't done any tricks in 3rd gear," said Ziny. "Tricks are not allowed on the interspace, Ziny. Zigzagging and swerving would be dangerous at 75 mph," replied Teacha.

"Well, what about 100 mph?" pleaded Ziny. "We can only drive that fast in outer space races and we won't be going into outer space until springtime. Come on, let's fly home," directed Teacha.

Ziny cruised home slowly in 1st gear. She switched her turbines to jumping gear and found a parking spot. Bouncing carefully into the space, she landed smoothly and climbed out of her Quasar.

"You have had an excellent first day, Ziny!" said Teacha. "Tomorrow we will go on a solar system field trip. Here is your key. Don't lose it! Your Quasar won't start without it."

Ziny took the key with a smile from ear to ear. It would go under her pillow for the night and she would dream about the trip. Tomorrow was going to be another great day!

Ziny's Driving School

Kindergarten- 3rd grade

Physical Education Standards Applied

Students will:
- Demonstrate a competency in the locomotor skills: hop, skip, gallop, slide, jump, leap, and jog.
- Demonstrate an understanding of pathways and levels. (Lesson 1)
- Demonstrate an understanding of cardiovascular endurance and interval training. (Lesson 2)
- Demonstrate communication and interpersonal skills in a game situation.
(Lesson 3)
- Actively participate in the movement portion of the lesson.
- Attempt to maintain movement during the entire lesson to increase fitness.
- Exhibit an understanding of self-space and safe speed while in motion.
- Enjoy movement and use self expression while pretending to drive a spaceship and to play with aliens.

Kindergarten- 3rd grade

Standards for Speaking and Listening Applied

- Confirm understanding of "Ziny's Driving School" when read aloud, by asking and answering questions about key details and request clarification if something is not understood.
- Ask and answer questions about "Ziny's Driving School" to gather information.
- Describe key ideas or details from "Ziny's Driving School" read aloud.
- Determine the main ideas and supporting details of "Ziny's Driving School" read aloud.

2nd and 3rd Grade

Literature, Informational Text and Writing Applied

- Ask and answer such questions as who, what, where, when and why to demonstrate understanding of "Ziny's Driving School".
- Use information gained from the illustrations and words to understand Ziny, Teacha, the setting, and the purpose of the story.
- Determine the meaning of general academic and physical education words and phrases in Ziny's Driving School."
- Determine the main idea of "Ziny's Driving School"; recount the key details and explain how they support safe movement and spatial awareness in the gym.
- Write a narrative to develop an imaginary experience on a new planet in our solar system using effective techniques, descriptive details, and clear event sequences.

Safety

Instructors will:
- Always announce the proper speed limit for the type of skill being performed.
- Stress that the students are to watch where they are going and maintain self-space at all times.
- Instruct the students to let go of the hoop if they feel themselves falling.
- Instruct the students not to stop in the middle of traffic. Students must move to the side of the gym to stop.
- Review the command for stopping (i.e. freeze, whistle blowing, etc.).

***Safety instructions included in this book are not meant to replace the discretion of the teacher. The teacher should implement any precautions deemed necessary. Children should be medically cleared for participation by a physician before participating in these activities.

Equipment

- As many hula hoops as there are children in the class.
- Music

Downloads

Jetson's theme song
Close Encounters
Star Wars
Star Trek
Superman
Greg and Steve's "Listen and Move" song on the *We All Live Together* CD

Lesson 1

First Day of School

Outline

- Read Ziny's Driving School.
- Tell the children that you will be Teacha and they will be the students learning to drive like Ziny.
- Give each child a hula hoop spaceship and have them spread out around the gymnasium. Instruct them to begin checking "landing gear" better known as hula hooping.
- Explain to the students that the area that their body takes up and all of the space as far as they can reach is their self-space.
- Explain that in order to stay safe, students must keep other people, objects, and spaceships from entering into their self-space.
- Tell the students to pretend they have a bubble around the Quasar and keep everything far enough away so that it doesn't pop.

Round 1

25 MPH

- Introduce the commands and demonstrate: 25 mph - walking while following the directions right turn, left turn, zigzag, swerve, high and low.
- Explain that 25 mph is used for crowded spaces when everyone is moving in
  different directions or if everyone is moving to the same place
  (i.e. lining up).
- Students begin walking with their hula hoop held waist level as a spaceship.
- Start the music and give speed and pathway commands.
- After a sufficient amount of time, stop the music and have students sit in their hoops.

Round 2

Black Hole

- Introduce the Black Hole - On the command, "Oh, no, a Black Hole" students will spin in their hoops from a high position to a low position and up again.
- Begin the music, give 25 mph commands and add the black hole.
- Stop the music and have the children sit in their hoops.

Round 3

Jumping, Hopping, Leaping

- Demonstrate jumping, hopping and leaping and use the following commands:
    "Oh, no a meteor shower! Begin jumping!"
    "Aliens crossing! Let's hop over them."
    "We're approaching the Milky Way! Try to leap over it."
- Begin the music, review the past commands and add jumping, leaping and hopping.
- Stop music and have students sit in their hoops.

Round 4
50 MPH

- Introduce commands and demonstrate: 50 mph - gallop, slide, skip.
- Explain that 50 mph is used in less crowded spaces. It could be with students moving in different directions or all in the same direction depending on the size of the gym.
- Review safety rules, start the music, and let students practice skills by reviewing and adding the new commands.
- Stop the music and have students sit in their hoops.

Round 5
75 MPH

- Introduce commands and demonstrate: 75 mph - jogging at 3/4 speed on the interspace highway with all students going in the same direction around the gym.
- Review safety rules.
- Start music and have students begin jogging in a clockwise direction.
- Stop the music and change directions.

Final Round
The Test

- Take students from 25 mph through 50 mph then to 75 mph and back down again.
- Finish with students stopping and putting down their landing gear (hula hooping).
- Have the students sit in their hoops and debrief.

Debriefing

Make the connection between the story and safe movement in the gym.
- What movements are at 25 mph? When should we use 25 mph? (Entering the gym and lining up to exit– crowded spaces.)
- What movements are at 50 mph? When should we use 50 mph in the gym? (Gallop, slide, skip– less crowded spaces.)
- What movement is at 75 mph? When should we use 75 mph in the gym? (Jogging 3/4 speed when we are all going in the same direction.)
- Can you move safely in the gym at 100 mph? (as fast as you can) (No, it would be too dangerous.)
- If a spaceship has a collision what could happen? (The spaceship might need repairs and the driver's lesson could be over.)
- If we have a collision in the gym what could happen? (Someone could be injured.)
- How do we prevent collisions from happening in the gym? (Always keep self-space, watch where you are going, move at a safe speed.)
- Should you ever stop in the middle of the gym to tie your shoe? Why not? (No, don't stop in the middle of the gym, someone could bump into you.)

Teacher's Role during Activity

- The teacher will be watching the students to determine when they have accomplished the task and/or show signs of fatigue. When the students demonstrate an understanding of the information given and/or are becoming fatigued, the teacher will stop the round and introduce the next round.
- The teacher will be looking for and making corrections to movement patterns and monitoring for safety.

Lesson 2

Ziny's Solar System Field Trip

Outline

- Welcome the students back to Driver's Education. Tell them they will be driving on the interplanetary highway to the different planets of the solar system.
- Point out that driving for long periods of time is good for the Quasar's turbines. Likewise, moving for a long period of time is good for the heart.
- Have the students "check their turbines" better known as feeling the heart beat or taking a pulse.
- Give each student a hula hoop and have them spread out around the outside of the gymnasium. Define an area to be called the interspace highway. (The area outside a volleyball court works best. If the gym does not have a lined area then place cones in a rectangle around the gym.)

Round 1
Mercury

- Explain to the students that they will be traveling to Mercury at 25 mph by walking. The time it takes to get there is 30 sec. Demonstrate that when the music starts they will travel clockwise walking. When the music stops, they will merge into the center of the gym and land on Mercury. To land, they will hula hoop and let it fall to the ground and sit in it. They will sit with hands folded in their laps.
- Begin music.
- Stop music after 30 sec. and have the students check their turbines. Ask them if they are beating fast or slow?
- Explain to the students that they have landed on Mercury.
- They will now leave their Quasar and step out onto the planet.
- Demonstrate that the creatures on Mercury jump like kangaroos. Have the students jump around the planet in and out of the craters (hula hoops).
- Have the students return to their Quasars and move back onto the highway.

Rounds 2-8
The Rest of the Solar System

Using the following chart, drive to each planet using the locomotor skill, speed limit, and time suggested. Land on each planet and have the students perform the activity described or make up their own.

Field Trip Guide

Planet	Locomotion	Speed	Time	Activity
Venus	Gallop	50 mph	30 sec.	Hop like Venetians
Earth	Slide facing the center of the gym	50 mph	45 sec.	Use hoop as a jump rope like Earthlings
Mars	Skip	50 mph	45 sec.	Spin hoops on their side like Martian pets
Jupiter	Jog	75 mph	60 sec.	Tip toe pretending to be the giants on Jupiter
Saturn	Skip	50 mph	45 sec.	Do push-ups like the strong people on Saturn
Uranus	Slide facing center of gym going the other direction	50 mph	45 sec.	Bear walk like the furry creatures on Uranus
Neptune	Walk	25 mph	30 sec.	Stretch like the rubbery people of Neptune

Reflections

- When were your turbines (heart and lungs) working the hardest, after walking at
  25 mph or jogging at 75 mph? (Jogging at 75 mph.)
- How could you tell? (My heart was beating fast! My pulse was a high number.)
- Explain to the students that just like a Quasar needs a lot of gas to go fast, muscles need a lot of air/oxygen to move fast. The heart has to beat fast to get the air we breath to the muscles.

Concepts to Teach
Interval Training

Explain to the students that just like there are different exercises to make arms stronger, there are also different exercises to make the heart stronger. Doing periods of locomotor exercises with short breaks in between is called interval training and is a great way to strengthen the heart.

Teacher's Role During Activity

- The teacher is starting, stopping and demonstrating the movements for each round.
- The teacher should be monitoring the students' exertion level. The time durations are estimates. Each grade level will have different times.
- Explain to the students that if they need to walk or stop they should do so closest to the outer wall.
- The teacher can and should use sound effects and give the creatures on each planet more character with a visual description. (i.e. The Martians are green with 6 eyes.)
- The teacher may also ask a student to describe what they see when they land on the planet and create the activity.
- The teacher should be reinforcing good effort and proper technique.
- The teacher should adapt language, concepts, and exercises to the students' abilities.
- The teacher should check heart rate/pulse periodically.

Lesson 3

Musical Craters

Outline

- Welcome the students to Pluto. Tell them that they are going to play a popular Plutonian game called "Musical Craters."
- Give each student a hoop and ask them to find their own space in the gym.
- Tell them that their own space is a space in which they can reach out and not touch any other person or thing in any direction. (K-1st graders will need to practice this a few times before they get the concept).

Part 1
Review of Skills and Speeds Without Spaceships

- Explain to the students that when the music starts, they will leave their crater (hula hoop) and travel around the planet.
- Discuss self-space. They need to keep a space around them as though they still have a spaceship.
- Demonstrate walking around the planet avoiding craters.
- Explain that when the music stops they will step into a crater and sit down.
- Start the music.
- Students walk around the hoops and sit in a hoop when the music stops.
- Perform a number of rounds with different locomotor skills emphasizing speed limits and moving with self-space without their spaceships.

Part 2
Cooperative Craters

- Explain to the students that when the music starts they will leave their crater and move as described.
- The teacher will remove a few hoops while the music is playing.
- When the music stops the students will find a crater. If they can not find one they must ask the inhabitant of another crater if they can share with them.
- Discuss how to introduce yourself and ask to share. "Hi, my name is Ziny. Can I share your crater?"
- Play as many rounds as necessary to review locomotor skills and speed limits.
- Keep removing hoops until everyone has a partner.
- Variation– Have students introduce themselves and share something about themselves (i.e. favorite color, pet's name, zip code, address, phone number.)

Reflection

- How did it feel when you didn't get a hoop?
- Was it hard to introduce yourself and ask someone to share?
- How can you help someone that is too shy to ask to share?
- Have you ever wanted to play something on the playground but were afraid to ask to play? Why were you afraid?
- If someone asks you nicely, "Can I play with you?" should you say yes or no?

Interdisciplinary Contests
2nd-3rd Graders

- Illustrations– Draw a picture of yourself on a new planet playing a game with an alien.
- Essay– Write a story about a new planet. Describe the people there, the environment, and what games or exercises they like to do.

Rubric

Pre-Control

1

Attempts at the locomotor pattern are discontinuous or do not resemble the skill at all.

Example: Student's attempts to skip consist of a hop followed by a few steps then a hop.

Developing

2

Locomotor skill has more correct elements but may be missing an element or they may be inconsistent.

Example: Student's attempts to skip consist of a step/hop with one foot but not with the other.

Mechanical

3

Locomotor skill is mechanically correct but is not one fluid motion.

Example: Student skips with exaggerated arm swing and/or heavy steps.

Fluent

4

Locomotor skill is mechanically correct and fluent.

Example: Student skips with a light smooth step/hop pattern.

About the Author

Lynn Hefele is a physical education teacher in the Huntington Union Free School District in Huntington, New York. She is the Vice President of the NYS AHPERD Suffolk Zone. A graduate of Springfield College in Springfield, Massachusetts, Lynn holds a Bachelor of Science in Physical Education and a Master of Science in Movement Science with a concentration in Biomechanics. She lives in Greenlawn, New York with her husband, Steve, sons, Harrison and TJ and their dog Buckets.

Lynn is the founder and president of Literature Enhanced Physical Education (LEPE, Inc.). She published "Clean Up Your Backyard" in 2009, "Ziny's Driving School" in 2011, "Cereal Soccer" and "Bugs and Bubbles in 2012, "Widget's Batting Lesson" and "P.E. Under the Sea" in 2013, and Swish in 2014.

Lynn manages the Linkedin group Elementary PE+, writes for PeLinks4u.org and is a member of the US Games Presenters Network.

References

Bruininks, Robert, Werder Sargent, Judy ,*Body skills: A Motor Development Curriculum for Children.* MN: American Guidance Services, Inc., 1988.

Couturier, Lynn, Chepko, Stevie, & Holt/Hale, Shirley. *National Standards & Grade-Level Outcomes for K-12 Physical Education.* IL: Human Kinetics, 2014.

EngageNY.org of the New York State Education Department. Common Core Curriculum. Internet. Available from https://www.engageny.org/common-core-curriculum; accessed September, 25, 2014.